ALL ABOUT
Coding Sequences

BY GEORGE ANTHONY KULZ

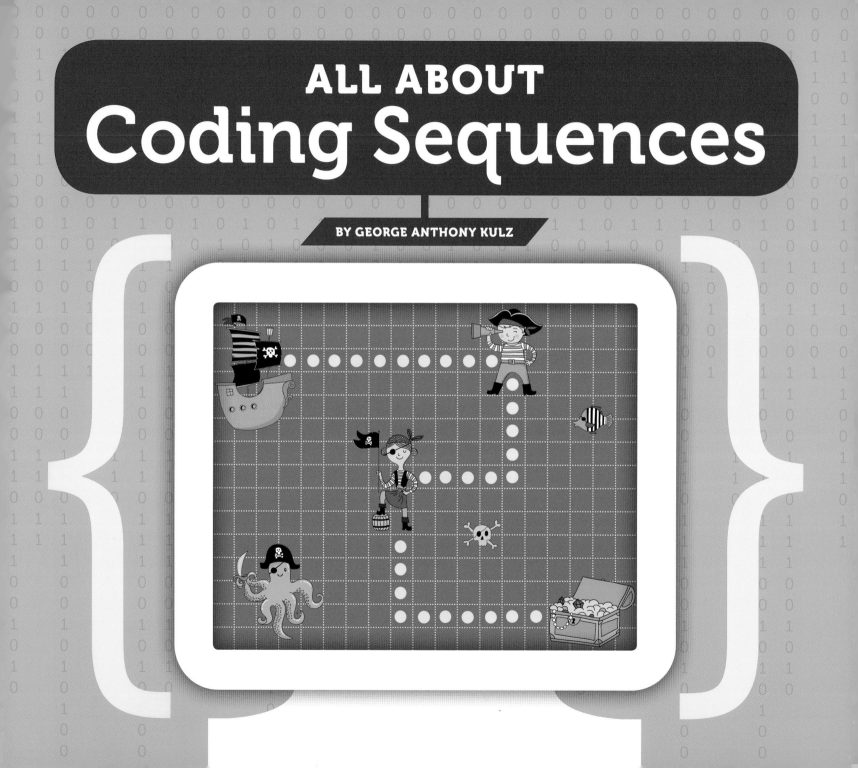

Published by The Child's World®
1980 Lookout Drive • Mankato, MN 56003-1705
800-599-READ • www.childsworld.com

Photographs ©: Shutterstock Images, cover, 1, 7, 11, 15, 16, 17, 18, 24; Maryna Kulchytska/Shutterstock Images, 5; George Rudy/Shutterstock Images, 13

ISBN 9781503831964
LCCN 2018962817

Printed in the United States of America
PA02418

ABOUT THE AUTHOR

George Anthony Kulz holds a master's degree in computer engineering. He is a member of the Society of Children's Book Writers and Illustrators and has taken courses at the Institute of Children's Literature and the Gotham Writers Workshop. He writes for children and adults.

TABLE OF CONTENTS

CHAPTER 1

What Is a Sequence?

Jack and Harriet look over Silverbeard the Pirate's treasure map. Jack picks up the shovel while Harriet reads the directions on the map.

First, they start at the shipwreck on the beach. Then, they walk 20 steps east to the trees. After that, they hop 30 paces north. Jack and Harriet look northeast through a spyglass to find the largest boulder. Behind that boulder, they find a secret cave. Once inside the cave, Jack digs a hole until he strikes something hard. Harriet scoops away the sand and pulls out a large chest. Inside is Silverbeard's long-lost treasure!

To find the treasure, Jack and Harriet had to follow the map's directions exactly.

Jack and Harriet found Silverbeard's treasure by following a **sequence** of clues on the map. A sequence is a set of steps that must be followed in order. If the steps are followed out of order, the correct results won't happen. The correct results also won't happen if any steps are skipped. Jack and Harriet would never have found the treasure if they had not followed the clues in the right sequence.

Just like a treasure map, computer **code** also has a set of steps that must be done in order. Code tells a computer what to do. The steps in code are called sequences. Sequences help computers do their jobs.

FOLLOWING A SEQUENCE

Here is the sequence of steps Jack and Harriet took to find the treasure.

Start at the shipwreck on the beach

Walk east 20 steps

Hop north 30 paces

Look northeast for the largest boulder

Find the secret cave

Dig

Uncover buried treasure!

CHAPTER 2

Why Is Order Important?

If a sequence must be written in the right order, what happens when the order isn't right? The result may look a little strange.

Suppose the following code steps are needed to draw a rectangle:

1. Draw a line from left to right 12 inches long.

2. Draw a line from top to bottom 4 inches wide.

3. Draw a line from right to left 12 inches long.

4. Draw a line from bottom to top 4 inches wide.

See the next page for how the rectangle would look.

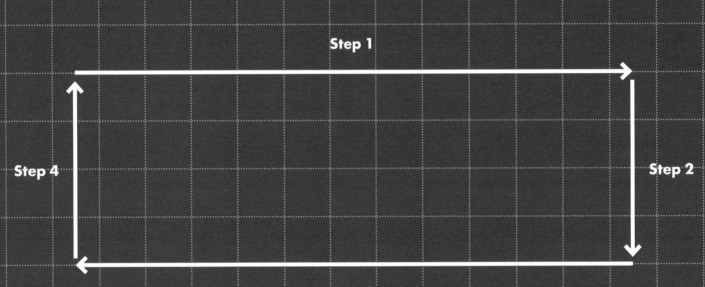

Step 1

Step 4

Step 2

Step 3

What if steps 2 and 3 were switched? The shape would no longer look like a rectangle. Instead, it would look like the picture below.

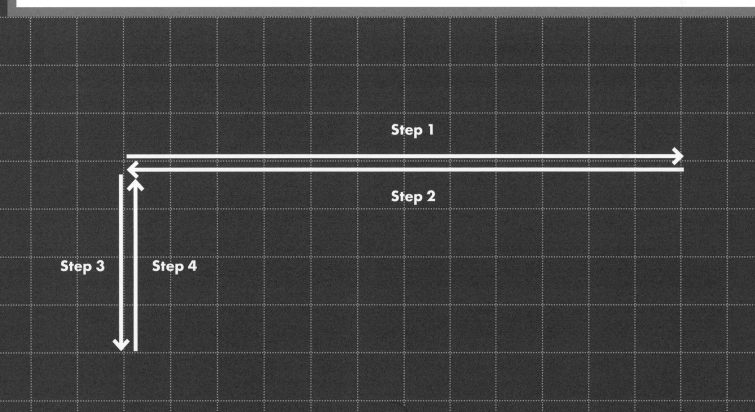

Step 1

Step 2

Step 3 Step 4

Clearly, the order of steps in a sequence is very important. Because the steps were not followed in the right order, the computer could not draw a rectangle. Sequences must follow the correct order or else they will not create the right result.

CHAPTER 3

What Do Sequences Look Like?

Sequences in code are written like a book. Books in English are written left to right and top to bottom. Code is written the same way. Sentences in a book are separated by periods, question marks, or exclamation points. Steps in code are often separated by special **symbols**. The symbols show where one step ends and another begins.

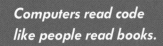
Computers read code like people read books.

Here is an example of code that finds the **area** of a rectangle:

```
length = 12; -- Set the length of the rectangle to 12 inches.
width = 4; -- Set the width of the rectangle to 4 inches.
area = length * width; -- The area of a rectangle is the length times the width.
-- This rectangle has an area of 48 square inches.
```

For the computer to find the area of a rectangle, the code first sets the length. The code then sets the width. Once the computer knows the length and the width, it can multiply them together to find the area. The ; symbol separates each step.

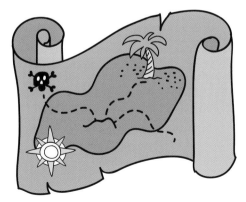

CHAPTER 4

Beyond Sequences

For some tasks, a simple sequence is not enough. Some tasks have more steps than a sequence can handle. Sometimes, a decision is needed, and sequences can't make decisions. Other tasks have steps that can go in any order. Some need actions to happen at the same time, but sequences can only do one action at a time.

```
}), b.on("click", ".bs-save,.bs-select-close
    console.log("save click V3")    refresh_log
}), b.find("select                              on()
}(function(a) {
    a.fn.custom_bt_select_checkbox = function(b)
        var c = a.extend({}, b),
            d = this;
        return d.each(function() {
            var f = a(this),
                g = !1;
            f.on("loaded.bs.select", function()
                g = f.parent();
                var j = !1;
                f.data("search_placeholder") &&
                var k = f.find("option"),
                    l = k.map(function(r, s) {
                        return {
                            t: a(s).text(),
```

Code can have many sequences. But sometimes the computer needs to do more than follow steps in order.

17

People use sequences with other types of code to solve more difficult problems.

When a simple sequence is not enough, it can be used along with other code structures. A sequence can come before, after, or inside these code structures. A **selection** is a structure that makes choices. A sequence can come before and after a selection.

A **loop** repeats actions. Sequences can be repeated in loops. In **parallel** code, more than one set of steps is followed at the same time. Sequences are an important part of solving problems with code.

Q: How are sequences written in code?

    a. top to bottom

    b. right to left

    c. left to right

    d. both a and c

A: d. both a and c

Q: Why do special symbols separate steps in a sequence?

A: Special symbols tell the computer where one step ends and the next one begins in a sequence.

Q: What is something a sequence cannot do?

    a. follow steps in order

    b. make decisions

    c. do two things at once

    d. both b and c

A: d. both b and c

Q: What happens if sequences are not followed in order?

A: If sequences are not followed in order, they will create the wrong result.

GLOSSARY

area (AYR-ee-uh) Area is how much space the surface of a shape covers. A computer can figure out the area of a rectangle by multiplying its length by its width.

code (KOHD) Code is a list of instructions that computers follow to do things. The computer follows code that makes it draw a rectangle.

loop (LOOP) A loop is a type of code that tells a computer to repeat an action. The loop kept drawing rectangles.

parallel (PAYR-uh-lel) Parallel means to happen at the same time or side by side. Parallel code makes the computer follow two sets of steps at the same time.

selection (suh-LEK-shun) A selection is a type of code that a computer uses to make a choice between different options. The computer used a selection to follow a different set of steps.

sequence (SEE-kwunss) A sequence is a set of simple steps in code that must be followed in order. The computer followed the sequence of steps to draw a rectangle.

symbols (SIM-bulz) Symbols are characters on the keyboard that are not numbers or letters. Special symbols like ; often separate steps in code.

IN THE LIBRARY

Claybourne, Anna. *Coding and Computers*.
Bath, UK: Parragon, 2016.

Woodcock, Jon. *Coding with Scratch Workbook*.
New York, NY: DK Publishing, 2015.

Woolf, Alex. *You Wouldn't Want to Live without Coding!* New York, NY: Franklin Watts, 2019.

ON THE WEB

Visit our website for links about coding:
childsworld.com/links

Note to Parents, Teachers, and Librarians: We routinely verify our
Web links to make sure they are safe and active sites.
So encourage your readers to check them out!

INDEX